Summer

Dog rose

Himalayan balsam.

Comfrey

Rosebay willowherb

Honeysuckle.

Foxglove

Common Mallow.

FOUR SEASONS

The Life of the English Countryside

FOUR SEASONS

The Life of
The English Countryside

Best wishes
Sheila Mannes-Abbott

The pictures of
SHEILA MANNES-ABBOTT
With text by
PHIL DRABBLE

EYRE METHUEN · LONDON

First published 1981
© Illustrations 1981 Sheila Mannes-Abbott
© Text 1981 Phil Drabble
Printed in Great Britain for
Eyre Methuen Ltd
11 New Fetter Lane, London EC4P 4EE
by W. S. Cowell Ltd
Ipswich, Suffolk

British Library Cataloguing in Publication Data

Mannes – Abbott, Sheila
    Four seasons.
        1. Country life – England – Pictorial works
        2. Natural history – England – Pictorial works
    I. Title. II. Drabble, Phil
    942'.009'734   S522.G7

ISBN 0-413-39920-6

FOUR SEASONS

The Life of the English Countryside

Spring is the time of year for sneaking up on shy creatures. The mixture of harsh winter frosts and intermittent rain breaks down the leaves into a soft, peaty sponge which muffles the clumsiest human footfalls.

By contrast, the shrill shrieks of unseen shrews, fighting for territory in deep cover, sound strident. Softer, rounded, more comfortable bank voles feed on fallen seeds or fragile shoots to bridge the gap between the rigours of winter and the promise of plenty in spring.

Later, in summer, those same voles may plunder my strawberry bed or rape my garden peas, but I bear them no grudge because they earn my respect as competent housekeepers, for they treat the hardest frost and deepest snow with a contempt that springs from their ability to emerge fat and sleek when others are feeling the pinch. At ground level, far beneath the surface of deep snow, they weave a maze of intricate tunnels and glean a harvest of fallen nuts and seeds, safely out of sight of hunting owls and stoats. Even after exceptionally harsh weather, which has decimated the populations of herons, woodpeckers, hares and shrews, a nucleus of voles always survives in triumph.

At the bottom end of April or early May, typical woodland butterflies such as the Speckled Wood appear. Less of a sun worshipper than most butterflies, and seemingly perfectly content to decorate the semi shade of clearings and woodland rides, its yellow or whitish spots on a dark brown background provide restrained beauty or almost perfect camouflage.

Grasses form the basis of the caterpillar's diet, so its habitat is not as confined to woodland as its name implies, but it is not always as well known that insects can be almost as territorial as birds. Anyone with a tiny suburban lawn can see the local robin chivvying off any other robin – even a member of the opposite sex – which casts covetous eyes on his patch, until ripening condition as the breeding season approaches highlights the fact that sexuality is not only a necessity for the survival of the species but very pleasant too.

So it is with many butterflies. Scientists who have daubed tiny patches of artificial colour on butterflies' wings and frequently recorded their position have discovered that they appear regularly only in the same rides and clearings, and that their territory can be plotted as accurately and as consistently as the well-defined territory of a mammal or a bird.

Spring Woodland

The countryside is not the countryside, for me, without rabbits. As a tiny child, I kept pet rabbits. As a youth, with my inseparable dog, and a ferret in my poacher's pocket, I caught them. As a grown countryman, I am lost in admiration at their sheer indestructability and powers of recovery in the face of natural catastrophe and myxomatosis, the worst disease developed and spread by evil men.

Farmers regard rabbits as pests, though I remember the days between the wars when farmers rode bikes instead of sitting in state in Range Rovers and rabbits were counted as a cash crop on many a marginal farm. 'Breeding like rabbits', of course, is no idle phrase, because every month of the year is their breeding season and they have the most marvellous method of birth control, devised by Nature to ensure the maximum chances of survival of their species.

The female comes on heat as soon as her young are born and is mated by the nearest buck rabbit. Each doe produces a litter about once every four weeks, by which time the last lot has been weaned. But to be perfectionists in propagation it is not enough to produce a litter at minimum intervals unless it is a litter of optimum size. So rabbits have a function called resorption. The embryos start to develop normally until about the size of walnuts, which is mid-term in the pregnancy. If the litter is smaller than the current food supply will support, the dam does not waste time in rearing them. They are simply resorbed into the body tissues, she comes on heat again and is immediately mated, in the hope that she will produce the 'right' number next time. Dominant does produce more than those lower down the social scale because their privileged position provides a better chance of rearing them. But, if too many are conceived, the surplus may be resorbed, because they might have jeopardised the chances of survival of their siblings. Rabbits, I feel, will survive when we are gone!

The arable fields of spring are green with promise and the chestnut 'sticky buds' are perfect for children to pick and put in jamjars on the window sill to watch Nature's slow motion film of the leaves unfolding before their eyes.

The different shades of green, in spring, are legion, and none more striking than the wild garlic – about which I have mixed feelings. It did me a marvellous good turn once when we were filming badgers and the stench of crushed wild garlic leaves where we had walked masked our powerful human smell, making the badgers oblivious to our presence. On the other hand, our hens loved the wild garlic that flourished in our paddock so well that it tainted their eggs, and I have no desire for such a Latin flavour with my breakfast!

Spring Wayside

Being no rarity-fanatic, I derive as much pleasure from a cock pheasant or mallard drake as from a golden oriole or Dartford warbler. Perversely, one of my boyhood ambitions was to have Swallow Tail butterflies at the bottom of my garden.

This was not entirely because they are rare, though they are only found wild in the low-lying fens of the Norfolk Broads, Suffolk and Wicken Fen in Cambridgeshire. Perhaps the main attraction for me was that Swallow Tail butterflies were among the first creatures – getting on for sixty years ago – to be regarded as threatened species by the general public. But Swallow Tails are still with us, and my ambition to see one in the wild is still unfulfilled!

This beautiful butterfly was once found in Kent, near London and as far north as Yorkshire and it is probably the destruction of its breeding habitat by modern farming methods – mainly land reclamation by drainage – that has caused the contraction.

Butterfly farms are now common and the eggs and larvae of many species of butterfly are freely available so, although the purists frown on people who introduce species which are not naturally indigenous or have not been recorded on the scientists' ten-square-kilometre maps, I should have more than a sneaking admiration for anyone who allowed a few Swallow Tails to 'escape' where parsley, fennel, wild carrot or angelica abound. The caterpillars will feed quite well in captivity on carrot, rue, parsnip or even ground elder. The over-wintering pupae emerge as butterflies in May or June and butterflies from the eggs they lay may be on the wing by August.

Being a Midlander, I never think of cuckoos as waterside birds because in my part of the country they mainly choose the nests of meadow pipit or hedge sparrow but, where there are large reed beds, reed warblers are common victims.

Young cuckoos hatched and reared by reed warblers or pied wagtails or robins are likely to choose a nest of the same species when they are old enough to lay themselves and, as cuckoo eggs vary considerably in colour to match the different host species, it is a great advantage to parasitise species which lay eggs of similar appearance. When the hen cuckoo sees her victim leave the nest, she flies down, takes the egg she wishes to replace in her bill, turns round and lays her own egg in the nest. She is often seen flying away with an egg in her bill, in order to dispose of it, and this gave rise to the belief that cuckoos put eggs into other birds' nests with their bills instead of laying them there, as actually happens.

Cuckoos, like reed warblers, arrive in spring and migrate in autumn. Sparrow hawks, which look very like cuckoos, are here all the time but are particularly shy in the breeding season, so our forefathers believed that cuckoos and sparrow hawks were the *same* birds, who were cuckoos in summer, when they were seen as well as heard, and changed into hawks in winter, when nobody either heard or saw a cuckoo!

Spring Waterside

No sight is more beautiful than a litter of fox cubs at play. They are at their best just before they are weaned, somewhere around Midsummer's Day, when their immature, woolly coats have moulted into sleek and shining fur that would add distinction to the slinkiest blonde. When they roll each other over in sham fights and stalk their unsuspecting brothers and sisters with mock murder in their hearts, their agility makes sluggards of the most graceful human athletes.

Their games are really serious rehearsals for the life-and-death struggles ahead, when they must capture food or die, and be equally capable of surviving the attentions of their arch-enemies, men with dogs or guns. Insidious snares and poison are hazards against which there is no defence but the ability to breed litters large enough – generally five or six cubs – to make good the losses.

Contrary to popular belief, foxes do not live all the year round in holes. When the weather is kind, they lie out in sheltered thickets or sunny hollows in reed beds. I have even seen a fox asleep right in the open, basking in the sun in the middle of a field of plough.

In spring, the vixen opens up several possible nurseries, sometimes traditional breeding earths, sometimes by enlarging a rabbit burrow, after eating the occupant, sometimes choosing a dry land drain or culvert. At first she suckles her litter but soon gives them their first solid food by regurgitating half-digested prey she has caught herself. As soon as they are mobile, at the age of three to five weeks, they play, and that is the time to watch them, if you can. The vixen brings food back to the den and there is always evidence of what they have been feeding on. A dried pheasant wing will be flicked in the air and caught with the grace and certainty of kittens; a rat's tail can seem positively attractive when used as a plaything. When they are ten or twelve weeks old the cubs are past this carefree, playful stage, and it is well nigh impossible to spy on them without their taking fright.

A few weeks after the fox cubs arrive, the fallow deer drop their fawns. They fawn in June, and the great majority of them in the third week. The timing is so regular that I have found it possible to make arrangements to film new-born fawns weeks in advance – and they have never let me down!

There is usually one fawn (roe deer often have twins) and, as soon as the doe has licked it dry and eaten the afterbirth, she suckles it and makes it lie down in a clump of cover, like a hare in a form. I have seen this happen dozens of times – but I still don't know how she gives the instruction! I believe it to be an oral squeak as it is certainly not any form of physical contact.

When the fawn is safely settled, its camouflage is so perfect that it is practically invisible and it lies so still, if strangers approach, that it would be easy to tread on it by mistake. The doe knows that her fawn is safer lying still than if it tried to run away from enemies before it was strong on the leg, so she leaves it alone for several days, only visiting to suckle it. While suckling, she licks under its tail, which stimulates it to defecate. The droppings are so charged with a mineral in which her diet is deficient that she eats them as they drop, which is a marvellous mechanism for ensuring that fawns, which are camouflaged safe from prying eyes, leave no scent either to betray their presence to prowling predators.

Summer Woodland

Rosebay willowherb is a survivor so it is not too choosey about its lodgings. It grows in woodland clearings and wayside verges, along canal towpaths and disused pitbanks. It was one of the first wild flowers to colonise the bomb craters and devastated building sites after the last war's air raids on London. But despite its apparent catholic tastes, its distribution is patchy. The fragile, downy seeds are blown by the wind but they need a bare patch of soil in which to germinate. There was a lovely lot in our wood, parts of which had been felled and replanted, enabling the rosebay seeds to grow in the bare patches of ground around the stumps. But the deer soon found the succulent herbage – and now there is none that deer can reach.

Rosebay willowherb has such summery associations for me, particularly because it is the favourite food plant of the Elephant hawk moth caterpillar. All the hawk moths are exciting. They are large, some of them very large, the Death's Head hawk moth, the largest insect in the British Isles, having a wing span of about five inches and its caterpillar being up to five inches long.

Stag beetles, Death's Head hawk moths and Swallow Tail butterflies are delights denied to Midlanders like me for they are localised to the east and south of England, Kent being particularly famous for Death's Heads and Stag beetles. But I have honeysuckle growing round my bedroom window – and Elephant hawk moths love it! I lie in bed on light summer nights, revelling in the sweet, heady scent and watching the Elephant hawks sharing my pleasure, hovering half an inch from a nectar-laden bloom and unrolling their delicate tongues to drink the nectar.

I am so fond of them because hawk moths and honeysuckle are the very spirit of summer for me, so I have fenced off a clearing in the wood especially to keep the deer out so that at least one patch of rosebay can flourish as a feast for the hawk moth caterpillars!

It was obviously the caterpillars that fired the imagination of the naturalist who originally put a name to the species, because the moth itself has a pointed body, and beautiful patches of mauve and puce on its wings, but the caterpillar has a lovely matt skin, precisely the dull grey of elephant hide. For me, idle summer days are poking about among patches of rosebay willowherb, looking for the great grey caterpillars hiding until nightfall, when they feed under the cover in clumps of willowherb. Or, on really sultry days, when the least effort is too great, I simply wait until teatime when the hawk moth caterpillars creep out of their hiding to sun themselves in the open. The mountain may not have come to Mahommet, but, if he had been a good naturalist, he would have found the wait for a visitation of Elephant caterpillars more rewarding.

Summer Wayside

My career as a naturalist was nearly nipped in the bud on the eve of my eighth birthday. Young newts and I share the distinction of starting life at approximately the same season and the one thing I liked better than catching newts was watching them breed in May in an aquarium which was the centrepiece of our breakfast table. In the excitement of wondering what present I was going to get, however, I forgot to put the top on the aquarium when I went to bed. Next day, the one thing I had not got was newts. Twenty of them cowered in crevices and under carpets and in every conceivable nook and cranny. It did nothing for my prestige!

But Great Crested newts are delightful creatures. Look at any picture of St George and you will see why they are associated with the dragons of folklore. Salamanders, which are somewhat similar reptiles and are still believed, by some European peasants, to be born in the heart of a fire, look as likely to breathe smoke as the dragon slain by St George.

In graceful courtship, the male newt cavorts, flaunting his brilliant yellow belly at his mate, as he twists and flexes his supple body. When the female spawns, she does not spout a shapeless mass of eggs, as frogs do, but produces a string, close-coupled as sausages and, when the chain gets long enough for her to reach down and grasp the end one, she uncouples it from its fellows as deftly as a prissy spinster taking off her gloves. These then hatch into tadpoles and, as the spring temperature rises, the whole metabolism speeds up so that gross feeding induces very rapid growth. Legs appear, but the tail is not absorbed, as with frog tadpoles, so they soon appear as perfect miniature newts. When taut skin will stand no more strain, it splits to allow the graceful reptiles to peel it off in a sinuous striptease, revealing a resplendent new skin to impart flamboyance to the next stage of the summer growth.

Small pools are best for newts because there is less chance of their being gobbled up by pike or perch or discovered by a heron. The eggs that the female detaches as she lays them are wrapped individually in the leaves of water plants, safe from the greedy eyes not only of sticklebacks and predatory beetles but of other newts as well.

Nothing even so small is safe from wild duck, though. The mallard, which winter in flocks on reservoirs and other large sheets of water, pair off in spring and choose, if they can, a small pool that they can have to themselves. There is then less competition from others of their kind for frog spawn and newt eggs, and for tadpoles and succulent newts as well, if they are not quick enough to avoid capture.

But the females have another reason for escaping from the flock. Mallard drakes are rumbustious lovers. The duck chooses a nesting site, to which she creeps at first light each morning to lay an egg. When she has laid, she drags a few leaves or blades of grass over the eggs to conceal them from thieving crows and magpies. As soon as she leaves her nest, the drake, who is waiting nearby, mates her.

When she has laid ten to fifteen eggs her clutch is complete and she goes broody and starts to incubate them, after which she is in no mood for love-making. Spring, however, has got into the blood of her mate, who is not famous for his fidelity. His wandering eye soon spots another duck leaving her nest after laying and he joins the queue of lovelorn drakes who chivvy and rape the decreasing number of females who have not completed their clutch.

Summer Waterside

The best way to see animals and birds in woodland is to sit on a comfortable log or to lean against a gate, staying motionless long enough to merge as a shadow into the surroundings. And the best time to do so is at dusk or dawn.

Autumn is the season to observe feeding hedgehogs. They give plenty of notice of their approach, for their protective spines give them the confidence to shuffle boldly along in search of slugs and beetles, vole nests and almost anything edible that presents itself. They rustle through the bracken and beech mast so loudly that they could be mistaken, in the silence, for distant children kicking up fallen leaves. Their manners are equally bad, for they smack their chops over anything they find, while the gourmandising crunch as they shatter the shells of banded snails is positively excruciating.

Their apparent gluttony, however, is a matter of need, not choice. Because their food supply ceases with the hibernation of slugs and beetles, they too must hibernate through the winter and, if they have not put on a heavy enough layer of fat, they will not live to see the spring. The sows often have a second litter and, if the young have not attained about a pound in weight by the onset of harsh weather at the bottom end of November, they have small chance of survival. If they are sleek and fat, the fat will be a deep yellow colour, devised by Nature as an eiderdown which can be gradually absorbed to avoid the necessity of replenishing the animals' food. They insulate themselves as well as possible with a deep covering of leaves, their surface temperature falls almost to air temperature and their breathing slows to several minutes a breath.

The sad thing is that their drive to feed is so insistent that they often haunt roadsides for beetles and insects that are stranded on the surface – and their misplaced confidence in the degree of protection their spines impart is such that they roll up in front of motor-cars instead of getting out of the way.

It is difficult to appreciate just what a puny harvest our farmers reap compared to the bounty provided for creatures in the wild. Every hawthorn hedge, in a good season, produces hundredweights of berries, which are scoffed by blackbirds and fieldfares, pheasants and wood pigeons, long-tailed field mice and short-tailed voles. My dog loves blackberries – and so do deer and foxes as well as the birds. In my part of the country, soil and climate are just right for damsons, and I often notice damson stones in fox droppings, ejected conspicuously on tussocks of grass or old tree roots, where other foxes will find them and decipher, from their highly scented language, messages of love from foxes of the opposite sex and hate from rivals.

Initially, it may seem strange for foxes to eat fruit but old Aesop obviously knew all about it when he wrote the fable of the fox and the grapes!

In every autumn oak wood there are literally tons of acorns, free for the gleaning by pheasants and deer, wood pigeons and rooks, wood mice and squirrels. Even the wild duck forsake their familiar waterside feeding grounds to go scrumping in oak woods for acorns and in beechwoods for mast. It is a marvellously profligate time of the year, when the whole of wildlife lives on Easy Street. By Christmas, they will have skimmed the cream and come down to reality with a bump that will drive in the lesson that Nature is a harsh mistress who has no time for weaklings, for there is scope only for survival of the fittest.

Autumn Woodland

I once employed a casual labourer to burn the 'lop-and-top' (the branches and leaves) left over when I had felled some trees to make a woodland ride. Never again! When I went to assess the work he'd done, I was horrified by the stark and naked trunk of a venerable oak that had been decently clad in a thick growth of ivy when last I'd seen it. My hackles rose and, when I spat out the question about what on earth he'd been doing, the poor fellow was grossly affronted. 'Ivy is a weed,' he patiently explained. 'It is a wonder it hadn't already strangled that valuable oak. No proper woodman tolerates ivy.'

What rubbish some genuine countrymen believe! It is honeysuckle which is the killer, not ivy. I have a lovely hazel walking stick with a spiral groove running up the side as neat and symmetrical as if it had been turned on the lathe of a master craftsman – except that the craftsman isn't born who could fashion such a spiral without destroying the bark. That groove was squeezed into the growing wood by Nature's tourniquet, a tendril of honeysuckle, which winds itself round a young, growing stem and refuses to give way to its host's demands for the latitude to grow. So the hazel grew taller and thicker except where the sweet honeysuckle hugged it in what would eventually have been a fatal embrace if I had not put it out of its misery by cutting it for a stick.

The ivy up my oak tree had been there for generations, clinging on but doing it no harm and providing, as a bonus, nesting habitat for countless birds, concealing young fledglings from jays and crows, though still leaving them vulnerable to agile stoats.

Stoats are among the most ruthless hunters in the countryside and will kill almost anything from a domestic barnyard hen to songbirds and small rodents. They are particularly fond of mice and voles, will often kill rats, especially young ones, and are devastating with ground-nesting birds, being particularly unpopular with gamekeepers because of their depradation of game birds.

Despite the enmity of sportsmen, however, stoats do plenty of good, for their favourite prey of all are rabbits, which are a scourge to arable farmers. They single one rabbit out and hunt him by scent as remorselessly as a pack of hounds, and the rabbits seem to realise this. I have seen large numbers of rabbits out grazing when one rabbit, hunted by a stoat, has run through the feeding group. They appear to appreciate that it is not *they* he is after and scarcely move aside. The wretched victim is in no doubt about his peril, and eventually sits in despair and squeals until the stoat catches up and kills him, although a rabbit could easily outpace a stoat if it only had the determination.

The description 'a bit of a stoat' for randy men is no exaggeration. The bitch stoat comes into season as her young are weaned and, although stoats don't pair in the conventional sense, dog stoats range wide in the rutting season and find and mate bitches in their post-lactation oestrus. While there, they also mate all the young females of the litter (in June or July), which do not then have their young until the following spring. Implantation of the sperm on the uterus wall is therefore delayed for about ten months before normal pregnancy begins.

Autumn Wayside

At our last house there was a mill stream which ran through a pool just by the dining-room window. At the back of the pool, no more than fifteen yards from the front door, banks of wild rhododendrons had been planted which had matured into a solid wall twenty or thirty feet high.

Kingfishers nested higher up the mill stream in deserted meadows and, every autumn, the young birds left their parents' territory in search of fresh fields. We first realised we had been honoured when we heard the characteristic shrill 'chickering' voices of two or three kingfishers which had chosen our rhododendrons as their autumn roost. Although their colour was brilliant by any standards, it did not have quite such an exotic sheen as old birds in full breeding plumage, so we always supposed that our visitors were young birds of the year exploring new territory.

It is astonishing what unlikely possibilities are investigated on these autumn forays and I have even found kingfishers perched on twigs beside the deep ditch that drains the centre of our wood, although the nearest continuous watercourse, a minor stream, is more than half a mile away. The ditch dries up in summer, so there cannot be fish for the catching, and I can only assume that the kingfishers prey on aquatic beetles which fly in from adjacent pools when autumn rains begin.

The dragonflies and dainty damozels could easily be relics of forgotten ages when dinosaurs and other prehistoric beasts held sway. Only the scale is different. There are forty-three species of British dragonfly, from tiny, iridescent damozels to huge creatures, several inches long, with four wings that rattle in flight, breaking the reverie of dreamers nodding off beside some limpid pool.

The adult insects do not look like conventional dragons, but their larvae do. They live below the surface of the water, sometimes for two years or more, and their huge, pincer-like jaws are the terror of creatures as large as newts and fish. As uncivilised lads, we used to introduce two dragonfly larvae to a jamjar of water and watch the ensuing battle as avidly as connoisseurs of fighting cocks. The object of each was to get a hold of its adversary with its great jaws through which it could suck the other's juices.

At this stage of their life history they look like miniature dragons as well as behave like them, but they then pupate and emerge as exotic flying insects which beautify the countryside from May to late September. Then they seem more like tiny helicopters than flying dragons and the ends of the females' bodies have protruding ovipositors to lay their eggs on submerged leaves and plants. Harmless as these are, they *look* like stings so that countryfolk slander them as Horsestingers.

Although horses have nothing to fear, other flying insects have. Each hunting dragonfly lays claim to a territory which it patrols, seizing smaller flying insects and eating them on the wing, discarding the dessicated shells when it has sucked their life juices. Macabre as it may sound, it is a primitive drama that never fails to grip me as I watch.

Autumn Waterside

The little owl, *Athene noctua*, as its name implies, is an introduced species which was so common near Athens that 'taking owls to Athens' had the same implications as 'carrying coal to Newcastle'. Specimens were introduced in several places in the last century, but the most successful results seem to have been near Oundle, in Northamptonshire, where they were liberated by Lord Lilford.

They are small birds, little bigger than a missel thrush, and are more diurnal than most owls, drawing attention to themselves by their plaintive, mewing cry. They are also conspicuous because they are mainly birds of open country, liking hedgerows and old park trees, and they often sit and sun themselves on telegraph poles, tree stumps and walls.

Because they have the typical hooked bills of hawks and owls, gamekeepers persecute them (illegally now), but careful research has shown that, as with hedgehogs, their bad reputation is undeserved. One scientist dissected many of the undigested food pellets they regurgitate and discovered that more than half their diet was composed of insects. The remains of 10,217 earwigs were found, with no less than 340 in a single pellet. They were also eating long-tailed field mice, voles and other small mammals and a few birds, but practically no evidence was found of damage to game. In my view, they are among the very few successful examples of introduced species.

Badgers, on the other hand, are truly native, truly woodland lovers and about the most nocturnal of our British mammals, although when summer nights are short it is possible to observe them feeding at dusk and dawn.

The dictionary term 'to badger' means to persecute unmercifully, and badgers have been snared, trapped and baited with dogs for generations. The Badgers Act (1973) was passed to prevent these malpractices but it proved worth hardly more than the parchment it was written on. Although it stopped badger-digging and gassing, it still allowed shooting and snaring by 'authorised' persons, which included landowners and anyone (including gamekeepers!) authorised by them.

But badgers came into the limelight more recently when the Ministry of Agriculture claimed that in the West Country they were spreading bovine tuberculosis. Ministry scientists inoculated a badger with a massive dose of TB and forced a calf to eat from the floor where the badger excreted. Not surprisingly, the calf caught TB. The experiment was reversed and a badger forced to eat from the floor where a tuberculous calf was urinating and excreting, so the badger caught TB. All that the experiments proved was that a susceptible animal can be infected by a diseased animal if the conditions are bad enough, but on this 'evidence' the Ministry has exterminated tens of thousands of badgers.

It is a policy that is doomed to failure because it has so often been proved that if any attractive area of habitat is denuded of a species it refills from the periphery as surely as water finds its own level. It would be far better if the Ministry scientists concentrated on producing resistance to TB in cattle by immunisation or other means.

Winter Woodland

Bullfinches are beautiful birds. They are also very destructive. The cock has bright pink cheeks and underparts. His chin, crown, nape, wings and tail are black and his white rump shows up clearly as he flits around in shady cover. His mate is similar but duller.

They love copses and thickets and well-shrubbed gardens and keep in contact with each other in dense cover by a low whistle that carries for a long way, though the formal, creaky song is unimpressive.

It is a pity that bullfinches do so much damage in orchards, but in spring they feed on bursting buds, wasting far more than they eat. A single pair will strip an apple or pear or plum tree till they ruin the chances of it fruiting, and they are just as devastating in the garden. In some areas they have been declared a pest and it is legal to trap or shoot them. I have some sympathy for commercial fruit growers, whose living may well be put in jeopardy by a population explosion of these birds, but I feel that gardeners can grow nothing more beautiful and birds have the added attraction of movement as well as delicate colouring. They will always find a welcome where I live.

The wood mouse, or long-tailed field mouse, is the most beautiful, graceful and agile of all our British mammals. It has a rich chestnut back, yellow flanks, white belly and enormous eyes and ears for its size. The tail is long and delicately tapered and the only other mouse with which it might be confused is the yellow-necked mouse, which is slightly larger, has a tail longer than head and body combined, and a chest spot that spreads into a yellow collar.

The size of eyes and ears gives the clue that wood mice form a major slice in the diet of many predators, so they need every aid to avoid capture. Foxes, stoats and weasels are partial to them and they form as much as 30 per cent of the diet of tawny owls in some areas. To minimise the risks, they make extensive burrows under woodland litter, emerging only at night to feed on berries and seeds and shoots, beetles, larvae and acorns. They spread to hedgerows and gardens and, in rural areas, they take up winter residence in outhouses and corn stores. A wood mouse, sitting on its haunches, twirling a grain of corn between its front feet to strip the husk and gnaw the kernel, is more delicate and graceful than the loveliest squirrel.

Although colour mutations are not very common, we have had a strain in our outbuildings for some years that are a delicate glossy peach, not quite white, but with the pink eyes of true albinos. To see them scaling rough walls and balancing on corn bin edges, with the aid of their long tails, gives me endless delight.

Winter Wayside

Although I spend more hours than most people in wild and secluded places, I can count on my fingers the number of times I have seen wild otters. This is partly because they are very shy and partly because they are, by nature, great wanderers, so that it is more difficult than with most animals to predict where they are most likely to be found. And this difficulty is increasing because otters are declining to the extent where the species is in danger of extinction in Britain, with the possible exception of remote Scottish islands and rivers.

The causes of the decline are poisonous pesticides, killing fish and frogs and thereby causing the death of otters by secondary poisoning; the destruction of their breeding holts in river banks in the cause of mechanised drainage; and increased disturbance by fishermen, boaters and walkers, who have more leisure to spend in quiet places and easy transport to get there.

Otters are mustilidae, having a musk gland under their tail, as have badgers, stoats, weasels, pine martens and polecats. This similarity has been known to scientists for many years but it seems to be less widely realised that the voice is also very similar, though of different pitch, to many of the other species. And the common posture of sitting vertical on the back legs to look around is almost identical to the familiar posture of stoats and weasels.

Otters are extremely playful and the sinuous ease with which they hunt under water gives place to equally beautiful play when several are together. They have a well-known habit of laying their front legs close along their bellies and sliding down a steep bank into the water. They like the sensation so much that they repeat the manoeuvre until a well-worn 'slide' shows clearly where their playground is, and they soon find a site for a fresh slide when they wander further up or down stream.

They do the same thing in snow and I was particularly interested to discover that a badger I was observing did exactly the same, though I have not seen this similarity in behaviour of the two species reported elsewhere. In the badger's case, however, the slide was not down a steep bank, as an otter's would have been. The badger literally ploughed a deep furrow as he rushed through the powdery snow and repeated the performance until it was smooth and hard enough to use as a slide.

Although the otter's characteristic 'whistle' is often referred to in literature – and can sometimes be heard a good way off, as a bitch calls to her cubs – it has a wide range of other vocabulary. At close quarters, otters can be heard chittering with anger or quarrelling over food, and they have a curious purr of affection, part way in pitch between a badger's whinny and a stoat's musical croon. But if a complete stranger heard the sounds without ever having seen any of the mustelids, it would be as natural to ascribe relationships amongst them as if their musk glands had been dissected in an autopsy.

Winter Waterside

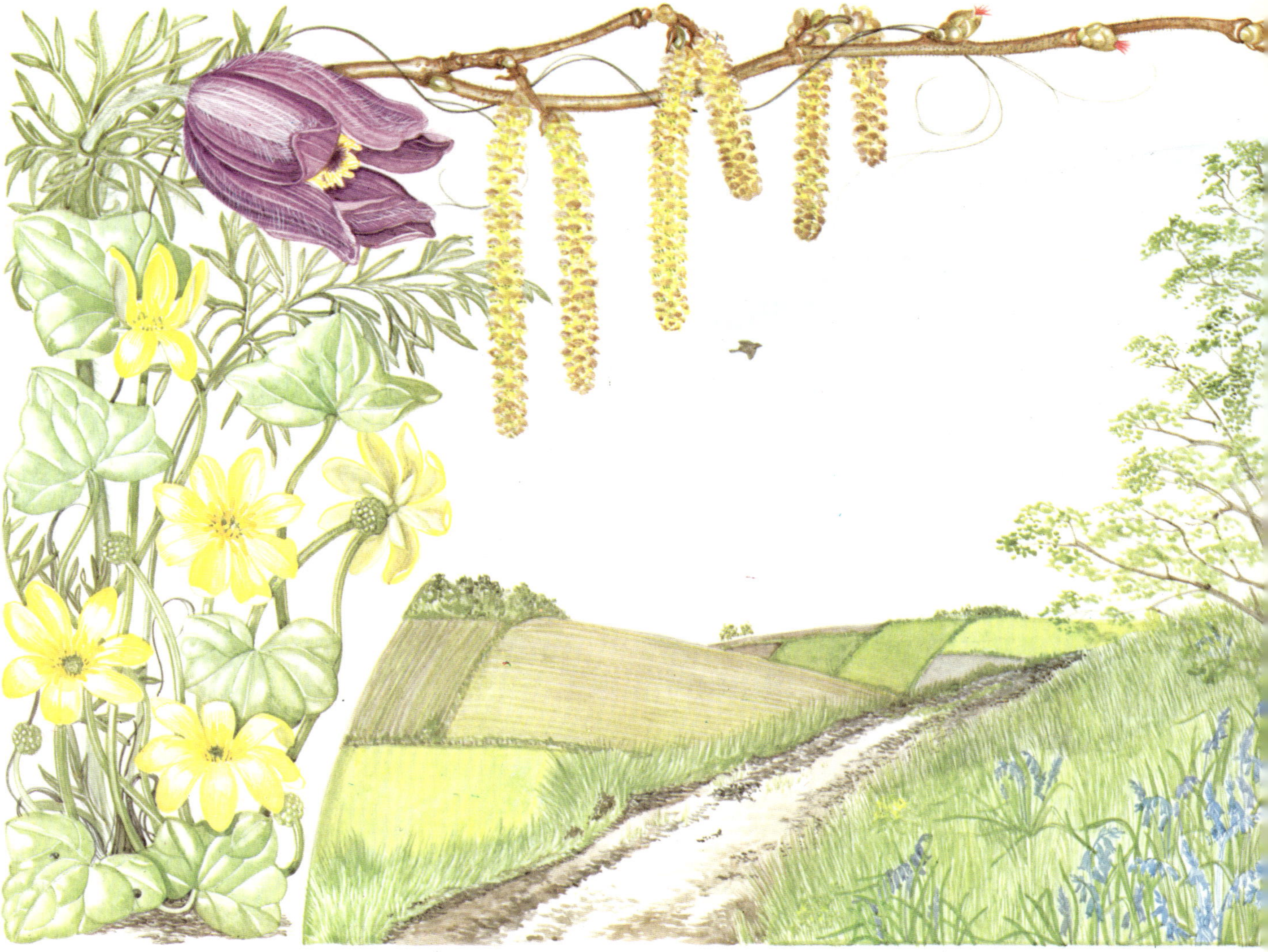

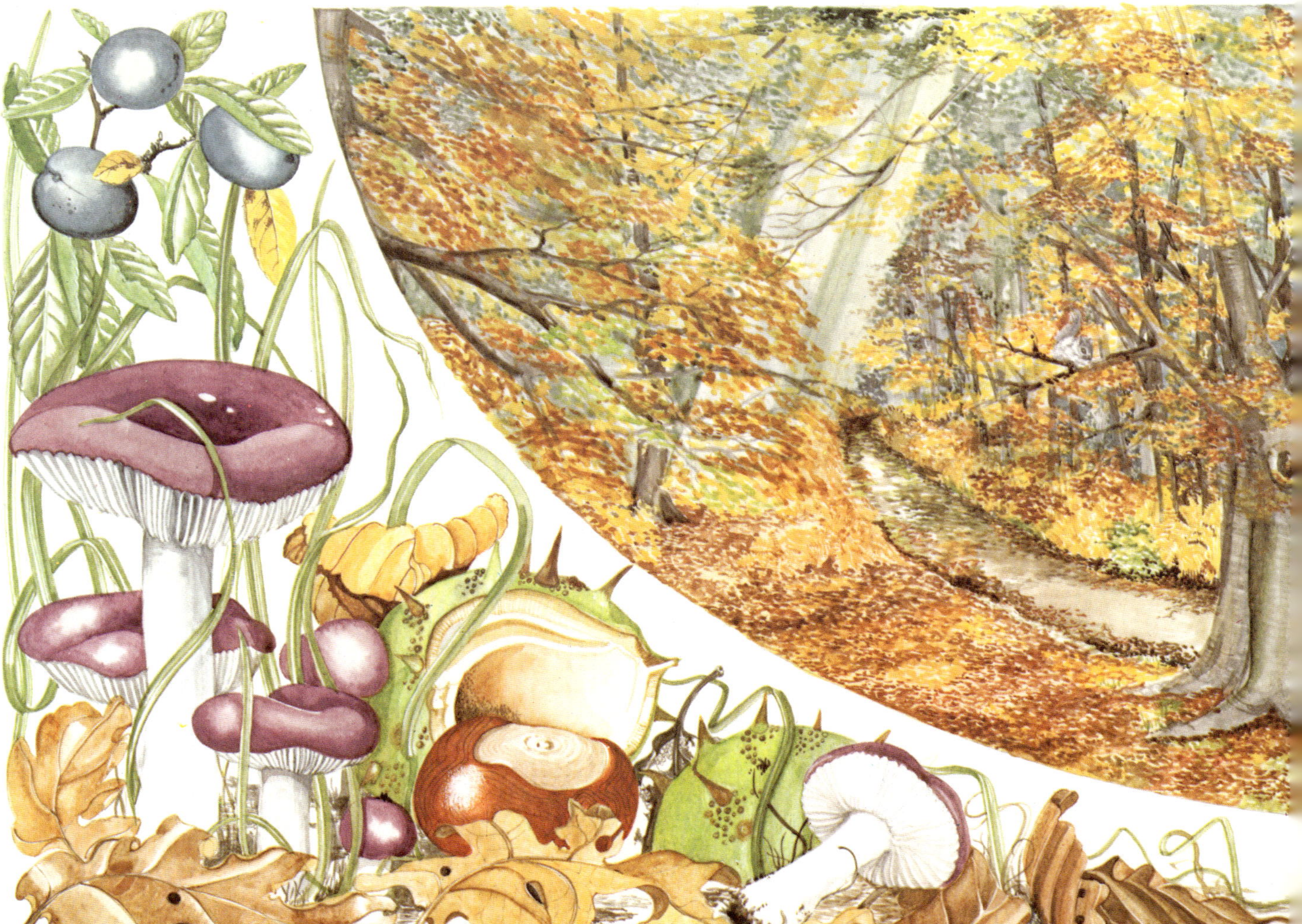

Acknowledgements

I should like to thank the following for their kind help in the preparation of my paintings for this book: Mrs Annabel Hillary, Dr J. Lorimer, Reading Museum, the late Professor Glyn Williams of the Department of Zoology, Reading University, and finally my husband, Edward Frewin, and my family for all their support.

The paintings in this book are my way of expressing and sharing with you my feelings for the countryside and the beauties of nature which are all around us by wayside and waterside and in the woodlands, but which are increasingly threatened by development and change. This was brought home to me when a small woodland near my home was itself threatened and my husband and I became involved, with the local preservation society, in trying to save it. I am sure many of you care as I do for wildlife and the countryside and I can do no better than commend you to join with your local Nature Conservation Trust in conserving the wildlife and wild places near your home. You can obtain full details of all the Trusts from the Royal Society for Nature Conservation, The Green, Nettleham, Lincoln.

Sheila Mannes-Abbott

Autumn

Sorrel

Dog rose hips

Bindweed

Bulrush

alder

Woody nightshade

amanita
muscaria

Blackberry

shaggy
ink cap

Ivy non-flowering shoots.